ANGER *the* *JESUS* Way

reflections
on the story of
Jesus healing
a man with a
withered hand
found in
Mark 3:1-6

Stephen Joseph Wolf

idjc.org

Dedicated to Father Ryan High School's
Humbert Aloysius "Pat" Corsini
who suffered my slow progress in the French language
while teaching me to love the good story

———————

Anger the Jesus Way
Copyright © 2016, Stephen Joseph Wolf
All rights reserved. No part of this book may be copied or reproduced in any form by any means without the written permission of the author.

Anger the Jesus Way, updated from *Anger-Grief the Jesus Way* published in 2009, is from conversations and prayer of a parish priest aware of an anger affliction, centered around a story in the Gospel of Mark, the only place where the gospel writers applied the word *anger* to Jesus of Nazareth. You might be as surprised as was the author.

Scripture texts in this work, unless otherwise noted, are taken from the *New American Bible, Revised Edition* (NABRE) Copyright © 2010, 1986, Confraternity of Christian Doctrine, Washington, D.C. and are used by permission of the copyright owner. All Rights Reserved. No part of the *New American Bible* may be reproduced in any form without permission in writing from the copyright owner.

The cover art icon by Stephen Joseph Wolf was given to the nursery chapel of Saint Stephen Catholic Community.

ISBN   978-1-937081-52-2
Ebook ISBN 978-1-937081-55-3

Stephen Joseph Wolf is a former parish priest, spiritual director, and retreat leader (22 lents & holy weeks) who before that worked as a certified public accountant (14 tax seasons), landscaper, desk clerk, laundry worker, janitor, paper boy, and student. In retirement, he volunteers as bookkeeper to two LGBTQ nonprofits, writes, paints, plays the ukulele, and lives in Nashville with his husband Billy.

IDJC Press books are printed and distributed by Ingram.   **idjc.org**

Anger the Jesus Way

	SONG *from* JESUS: *As Abba Loves Me*	4
I.	**Introduction: The Story**	5
	A Prayer for Experimenting & Editing	13
II.	**Watched in the Sabbath Assembly**	15
	A Prayer for Myself when Visited by Anger	25
III.	**Invited by Jesus**	27
	St. Benedict's Twelve Steps to Humility	35
IV.	**Riddle Silence**	37
	A Forgiveness Model	43
	A Prayer for an Institution	45
	EZEKIEL SONG	46
V.	**Anger-Grief**	47
	In Health & In Healing and *31 Days of God's Love-Call*	55
VI.	**Turning to Freedom**	59
	Loving Abba, This is my brother	60
	My Beloved	67
	Taking Anger into the Trinity	69
	Sources and For More	70
	Thanks That Be	74

A SONG *from* JESUS

Text: from John 15, Stephen J. Wolf, 2007, public domain
tribute to the priesthood of Charley Giacosa
Music: BUNESSAN 5554 D, Scots Gaelic melody
Popular melody for *Morning Has Broken*

As Ab-ba loves me so do I love you.
I tell you this: re-main in my love.
Keep this com-mand-ment: Love one an-oth-er
As I have loved you, call-ing you friend.

I am the vine and you are my branch-es;
Let Ab-ba prune you so you bear fruit.
My word re-mem-ber: Love one an-oth-er
As I have loved you, call-ing you friend.

No great-er love has one than to lay down
One's ver-y life for e-ven a friend.
You I have cho-sen: Love one an-oth-er
As I have loved you, call-ing you friend.

You have been with me from the be-gin-ning;
Tes-ti-fy in the Spir-it of truth.
In word and ac-tion: Love one an-oth-er
As I have loved you, call-ing you friend.

I
Introduction: The Story
Mark 3:1-6

1   Again Jesus entered the synagogue.
        There was a man there
        who had a withered hand.

2   They watched him closely
    to see if he would cure him on the sabbath
        so that they might accuse him.

3   He said to the man with the withered hand,
        "Come up here before us."

4   Then he said to them,
    "Is it lawful to do good on the sabbath
        rather than to do evil,
    to save life rather than destroy it?"
        But they remained silent.

5   Looking around at them with **anger**
    and grieved at their hardness of heart,
        he said to the man,
        "Stretch out your hand."
    He stretched it out and his hand was restored.

6   The Pharisees went out and
    immediately took counsel with the Herodians
        against him to put him to death.

Sabbath is the day of the week. Jesus is in the synagogue in Capernaum. Others are there, including some pharisees and a silent man with a withered hand. Jesus knows the pharisees are wondering if he will break the law again by healing on the sabbath. He asks them a riddle, to engage them in dialogue. They remain silent, refusing to talk to him. He turns to them in **anger** and grieves over their hardness of heart. He then asks the silent man to stretch out his withered hand, and it is healed. The pharisees go out to make plans how best to kill him.

The Son of God experienced human anger. He was aware of the unhealed or willful blockage in the pharisees that kept them from entering into dialogue with him. God invites and cajoles, but God does not violate our freedom.

So in his humanity, Jesus feels the emotion of anger. He does not go looking for it, but it finds him. In his divinity he loves even these pharisees. He wants to engage them in some kind of healing dialogue, but they refuse in stubborn silence. He acknowledges to himself this human emotion of anger, and then holds it with grief, with divine compassion. He suffers with the pharisees who are still unhealed, still blocked.

Introduction: The Story

The story itself is one of those readings in our three-year Sunday Lectionary cycle often omitted, knocked out by an early Lent (Mark 3:1-6, on the Ninth Sunday of Year B, Ordinary Time). So it is a story we hear on Sundays less than once every three years. And it is not chosen for special feast days.

In Chapter 3, Verse 5, of the Gospel according to Mark, we have the only passage in the New Testament in which we are told that Jesus experienced the emotion of anger.

What might this story hold? I have been told that depression is anger turned inward. I know something about depression, the way you know something about your cross. You know, the one you have been called by Jesus to pick up daily and carry while following him.

I suppose my depression cross is why they invited me in the seminary to take a look at my "anger issue." I had to admit it. I have an anger issue. I have my sainted mother's Scotch-Irish temper. But I was a holy seminarian! How could they tell I had an anger issue?

No matter. Full of the eager glow of a Bible student with a new quest, I headed straight for the library concordance. *Concordance*. A new word in my vocabulary. The concordance would give me a list of every use of the word *anger* (or *angry*) in the Bible.

I wanted to know something about Jesus and anger. Only one passage applied:

> ...*looking around at them with **anger**...*   Mark 3:5

Surely this was not the only passage that used the word anger or angry and applied it to Jesus! What about, you might be thinking as I was, what about Jesus cleansing the temple? He drove them out with a whip! I know he was angry that day!

So I read all four accounts of the temple cleansing scene: Mark 11:15-19; Matthew 21:12-13; Luke 19:45-46; John 2:14-16. John's version skirts closest to anger, but we're told he went to the trouble of making a whip. When I slow down to be a craftsman, my anger usually slides away in the work. But John does mention the whip, a weapon:

> *...Jesus went up to Jerusalem.*
> *He found in the temple area*
> *those who sold oxen, sheep, and doves,*
> *as well as the money-changers seated there.*
> *He made a whip out of cords*
> *and drove them all out of the temple area,*
> *with the sheep and oxen,*
> *and spilled the coins of the money-changers*
> *and overturned their tables,*
> *and to those who sold doves he said,*
> *"Take these out of here,*

and stop making my Father's house a marketplace."
His disciples recalled the words of scripture,
"Zeal for your house will consume me"

John 2:13b-17
Zeal is from Psalm 69:10.

Zeal. Not the same thing as anger. Experiment with this passage in your imagination. In John, this is right after the first sign at the Cana wedding. Pretend that Jesus knows fully well that it is time to draw some attention to himself and begin challenging the status quo. Imagine that Jesus knows that in the progression of his ministry those with power and authority would have to get riled up at him. Knowing that some anger among them was inevitable, what if Jesus had the most enjoyable day of his three years of teaching and preaching and healing? Have you ever pushed your best friends' buttons, just to rile them up, just for fun, or even for their own good?

When my seven brothers and I were young boys, and one of us would ask our father, "Hey Deddy (We spelled "Deddy" the same way we said it.), why are you doing this?" His favorite non-answer was "funzies," just for fun. Praying once with one of these temple passages, I watched Jesus fashion a whip to use, looking at me with a face expressive of "watch this!" I had already read the passage, so I knew the purpose of the whip. When I asked Jesus why, he answered, "funzies." Like a parent trying to discipline a child, or a friend at play with a practical joke, Jesus could not let them see him laughing inside. So the effect on the crowd was the same. Inside jokes can be the best, and zeal can be funny too.

Well, what about when Jesus rebuked Simon, even calling him Satan! Surely Simon made him mad! In Mark, this happens after the first of three predictions of Jesus' coming passion and death.* We are told simply that Simon *rebuked* Jesus and that Jesus then *rebuked* Simon, looking at his disciples saying,

> *Get behind me, Satan.*
> *You are thinking not as God does,*
> *but as human beings do.*

* Mark 8:31-33; see also Matthew 16:21-27; Luke 9:22-26.

In Matthew, Jesus also calls Peter *an obstacle* to him. Luke lets his friend Peter off the hook, leveling the *rebuke* by Jesus against all the apostles, directing them to tell no one who Jesus is. Again, as in the cleansing of the temple, Jesus may indeed have been angry with Peter, but the gospel writers do not use that word. The setting and the tone suggest *anger*, but the word is not used.

And this is my point in this introduction:

The gospel narratives do tell us, with the word, that Jesus was angry, but only once, and by only one gospel writer (Mark), and in only one episode (3:1-6, the story of the healing of the man with a withered hand). It is certainly reasonable to say that, in events similar to the cleansing of the temple and Jesus' rebuke of Peter, our Lord was angry, and that those around him knew he was angry. All four gospel writers, including Mark, choose to not use the word.

But why is the word used in this particular passage? Why in this specific story? Might the Holy Spirit be trying to tell us something in this explicit account of the human anger of Jesus the Christ? I think so, and I think I know what.

What I wish to propose is an intimate connection of his anger in this story with the core teaching of Jesus from his great sermons:

A.	*Love your enemies...*	Mt 5:44; Lk 6:35
B.	*Pray for those who persecute you...*	Mt 5:44
C.	*Forgive...*	Mt 6:14; Lk 6:37

Some wish to dismiss these as the *too hard teachings* of Jesus. His anger tells us that though he also did not always find them easy he nonetheless taught them as both necessary and healing.

SOME QUESTIONS *for* PONDERING

1. Have I ever been angry with...
   - someone causing a commotion at worship?
   - a religious leader?
   - a lawbreaker?
   - a riddler?
   - someone insisting on talking?
   - someone refusing to talk things over?
   - someone with a hard heart?
   - someone blessed with blessings?
   - someone who is planning violence?
   - God?
   - myself?

2. One definition of the word *dialogue* is an exchange of ideas and opinions between two or more people. Why is it so hard to have an honest dialogue while angry?

3. Have I ever wanted God to violate my free will?

4. How can I recognize anger turning inward?

5. If I compare my spiritual life to the rooms of a house, is there one Jesus wants to clean up?

6. Is it possible to rebuke someone without being angry?

7. What do I think about the idea of anger as an emotion or a feeling that happens to us? Can I make a distinction between being angry and what I do with it?

A PRAYER *for* EXPERIMENTING *&* EDITING

Lord my God,
it has happened again and anger is visiting me.
I hear also your gospel call to love enemies,
to pray for persecutors, and to forgive.
Because I trust in your way I pray:
I am angry right now with *N*.
Judging is your job alone
for you alone have all the data.
Like me, *N*. is created in your image
and loved by you without limit.
But there seems to be something unhealed in *N*.;
I know not what it is,
and *N*. may not know either,
but you, Lord, you know:
and I believe that you want to heal it.
This I ask you to do.
Lay onto *N*. your healing touch.
Amen.

A SONG *from* JESUS

Text: from John 15, Stephen J. Wolf, 2007, public domain
tribute to the priesthood of Charley Giacosa
Music: BUNESSAN 5554 D, Scots Gaelic melody
Popular melody for ***Morning Has Broken***

As Ab-ba loves me so do I love you.
I tell you this: re-main in my love.
Keep this com-mand-ment: Love one an-oth-er
As I have loved you, call-ing you friend.

I am the vine and you are my branch-es;
Let Ab-ba prune you so you bear fruit.
My word re-mem-ber: Love one an-oth-er
As I have loved you, call-ing you friend.

No great-er love has one than to lay down
One's ver-y life for e-ven a friend.
You I have cho-sen: Love one an-oth-er
As I have loved you, call-ing you friend.

You have been with me from the be-gin-ning;
Tes-ti-fy in the Spir-it of truth.
In word and ac-tion: Love one an-oth-er
As I have loved you, call-ing you friend.

II
Watched in the Sabbath Assembly
Mark 3:1-2

1   **Again Jesus entered the synagogue.
There was a man there
who had a withered hand.**

2   **They watched him closely
to see if he would cure him on the sabbath
so that they might accuse him.**

Again. Jesus had crossed this threshold for what, thirty years? How many sabbaths is that? There was a day when he could do so as one of the crowd, hardly being noticed. Not any more, unless he is able to go into a church, synagogue or mosque in this third millenium without being noticed. Do Christians hold him to his promise in Matthew 18?

> *For where two or three* (or more?)
> *are gathered in my name,*
> *there am I in the midst of them.*
>
> Matthew 18:20

If two is company and three is a crowd, then two is also private, and three (or more) is public. When we gather in the name of Jesus, whether in private or in public, there he is, in our midst, a real presence. Is this why our liturgy calls for an Opening Song, to proclaim out loud *both* that we are gathered in his name and that God-is-with-us (*Emmanuel*)?

We are told that he was in the *habit* of entering the synagogue. It is said that forming a new habit takes 40 times, or 28 days, or 6 weeks, before the thing is no longer new, but ingrained. Entering the assembly is what Jesus did, and what Jesus does.

The synagogue service was not the same as the temple sacrifices, synagogues having been built wherever there was a community of faithful Jews, and there being only one true temple, the one in Jerusalem. Since early in the first millenium, there have been four parts to the Christian Sunday liturgy:

1. We are gatherd.
2. The word is proclaimed and heard.
3. The breaking of the bread.
4. We are sent on mission.

Liturgists have compared the synagogue service of the time of Jesus and Mary and Joseph with our *Liturgy of the Word*, and the temple sacrifice of Jesus' day with our *Liturgy of the Eucharist*.

Our very word "Church" is a translation of the Greek word *ekklesia* (Matthew 16:18;18:17), for the Hebrew word for the assembly of the chosen people in the forty years of desert pilgrimage from Egypt to the Promised Land, after being led out of slavery and before being led into freedom. Our church wanders, but as pilgrims, not nomads. As with the Chosen People in the exodus, God has for us a destination.

An important distinction is that our Sunday is not the sabbath day of rest marked by our Jesus, the faithful Jew, or for his disciples and apostles in the earliest days of the church. Since the sabbath, the seventh day of the week, was the day of rest for the people of Jerusalem, the experience of the earliest churches might have been similar to us taking the day of rest on Sunday, and then going to weekly Mass before going to work on Monday. I am told that just a couple of generations before me, many Catholic Irish in Nashville had to work on Sundays, and so would attend the dawn mass at Cathedral of the Incarnation, and then go to work. Is their experience all that different from that of early Christians or third millenium immigrants?

It is important for Christians to remember that we do what we do on Sundays *on Sunday* because Sunday is the day on which Easter happened, the first day of the week. Every Sunday is another Easter, and it is the resurrection that makes all the difference.

But back to Jesus of Nazareth, now of Capernaum, who enters the synagogue with everyone's eyes upon him. Their eyes are also on another: a man there who has a withered hand.

There are two problems:
1. The man has a real disability, just like others who have already been healed by Jesus.
2. The decalogue: *Remember to keep holy the sabbath day* (Exodus 20:8), the day of rest.

Is it the man's right hand or left hand? We are not told. We can presume that it is a problem for him, for if the withered hand was not experienced by the man as a problem, why would he need a cure?

The problem may be as simple as the daily competition of the day-laborer. We are told in the previous passage that the fields of grain are ready with heads of grain. With only one good hand, he would be one of the last harvest-workers to be hired. He would only be hired if there was a shortage of workers, and he would not be able to harvest as much grain as other workers. When times are difficult and a day-laborer is not hired, it may come down to no work means no pay, means no food to eat, or the indignity of being a charity case.

We are not told whether the withering has been for his whole life or a recent affliction. It really does not matter. Jesus has already been healing many people. Clearly this man's withered hand is suitable matter for the ministry of Jesus.

We are also not told that the man asks to be healed, or that he has a friend or family member who makes the request. Perhaps this is an indication of the isolation that his malady has brought upon him.

So what about the hand? I have an early memory of doing simple yard work with Momma and some of my brothers. It was at the old house, so I was no older than ten. I wanted the hoe being used by a brother, and said so. Momma paused in her work, and after a quick look told me to just use my hands. My hands? She told me to look at my hands and said, "Nobody has invented any tool better than those two that God has already given you." My hands became a treasure.

A parishioner missing one of his thumbs once told me that most people have no idea what a gift it is to have "opposable digits." What kinds of stories might this silent synagogue man be able to tell of how one hand, be it withered or be it healed, can make a huge difference? He has almost certainly felt judged by this verse from the Babylonian Exile:

> *If I forget you, Jerusalem,*
> *may my right hand wither.*
>
> Psalm 137:5

I have a friend who once told someone "In me, you have an enemy to the grave!" My friend died. At the funeral visitation, another friend wanted to remind the man to whom those words had been spoken that, "he's not in the grave yet!"

Do you know someone who might presume to consider himself or herself to be your enemy? Is there someone you sometimes consider to be your enemy? If I directed this question about you to your spouse, boss, doctor, lawyer, mother, son, business partner, golf buddy, bunko sister, massage therapist, dentist, barber, hairdresser, brother monk, sister nun, closest neighbor or best friend, would one of them be able to help you name that person? (I sometimes ask the child who can't think in the confessional of even one sin, "is there something your mother might want you to remember right now?") Reflect on a time in your life when you experienced having an enemy. How did that come about?

There is always a background story. Here is the background for our Anger story:

Back again to Jesus, who enters the synagogue with everyone's eyes on him. We are still early in the concise account of *the gospel of Jesus Christ the Son of God* (Mark 1:1). Already Jesus has been baptized in the Jordan by John, hearing the voice from the heavens: *You are my beloved Son; with you I am well pleased*; been driven by the Spirit into the desert for forty days and been tempted; begun to proclaim in Galilee *the gospel of God:* *This is the time of fulfillment.*
The kingdom of God is at hand.
Repent, and believe in the gospel.   Mark 1:15

He has called the two sets of brother-fishermen: Simon and Andrew, James and John; in Capernaum on a sabbath he cured a man with an unclean spirit and Simon's mother-in-law, and after the sabbath-ending sunset cured *many who were sick with various diseases* (1:34), and he drove out many demons.

After a very early morning of prayer, he left Capernaum, but cleansed a begging leper, who then *began to publicize the whole matter…so that it was impossible for Jesus to enter a town openly.* He stayed in deserted places, but *people kept coming to him from everywhere* (1:45).

After some days, Jesus went back to Capernaum and we have a sort of shift in the tone, where Jesus becomes more provocative.

Word spread, a crowd gathered, and he *preached the word to them* (2:2). Into the middle of this a paralytic is carried by four men, whose faith inspires Jesus to say to the paralytic,

Child, your sins are forgiven. (2:5)

Now he has the attention of *some of the scribes* there, who begin asking each other if Jesus is blaspheming. We are told that Jesus knows *in his mind what they* are *thinking to themselves* (2:8). He asks them a rhetorical question, and without waiting for a response declares

> *that you may know*
> *that the Son of Man has authority*
> *to forgive sins on earth*
> he says to the paralytic,
> *I say to you, rise,*
> *pick up your mat,*
> *and go home.*

The paralytic does as Jesus said, and all are astounded. The crowd follows him along the sea, and he teaches them. He calls Levi, who leaves his customs job and feeds Jesus in his own house. Some scribes who are pharisees see Jesus eating with sinners and tax collectors, and challenge not Jesus but his disciples. Jesus himself hears their questioning and responds,

> *Those who are well*
> *do not need a physician,*
> *but the sick do.*
> *I did not come to call the righteous*
> *but sinners.* (2:17)

When people question Jesus about his disciples not fasting as did the disciples of John and the pharisees, Jesus answers with parables of wedding guests with the bridegroom and new wine in new wineskins. When Jesus teaches in parables, we know there are always multiple layers of meaning.

The pharisees themselves then challenge Jesus directly with the bad example given by his hungry disciples, who pick heads of grain ("work") on a sabbath while walking through a field. He responds with the unimpeachable example of King David himself and his companions, who violated the law by eating the bread of offering in the house of God, and then gives them this blunt mystery:

> *The sabbath was made for man,*
> *not man for the sabbath.*
> *That is why the Son of Man*
> *is lord even of the sabbath.*
>
> Mark 2:27b,28

This language is very dangerous to a whole way of life built not just on the Torah, but around all kinds of other rules of life. If the weekly observance of the sabbath was up for grabs, what would be next? If the *scribes who are pharisees* have a response to what Jesus has just said, we are not told it.

So here we are again in the synagogue on another sabbath. Jesus enters again.

SOME QUESTIONS *for* PONDERING

1. To judge is the job of God alone, who alone has enough data. If I judge someone for judging another, does that make me a pharisee?

2. To what extent is my *acting out* in anger a habit I have let grow? What contra-habit might help?

3. How do I feel called to keep holy the sabbath?

4. Frederick Buechner commented that anger is *in many ways a feast fit for a king. The chief drawback is that what you are wolfing down is yourself…*
If the awareness that my anger is chiefly doing harm to **me**, why is that awareness not enough to banish it?

5. Does the tension-building background story on pages 21-23 shed any light on the anger of Jesus in Mark 3:5? Is there a *slow-burn* happening?

6. *It is easy to fly into a passion — anyone can do that — but to be angry with the right person to the right extent and at the right time and with the right object and in the right way — that is not easy and it is not everyone who can do it.*   - Aristotle

   How wise is the philosopher Aristotle? Might his teaching hold a kernel of the gospel?

7 In the *Penitential Act* of the Catholic Mass,
we are invited to call to mind our sins and
express our sorrow and hear a priest's words of
"absolution" before participating in the *Liturgy of the Word* and the *Liturgy of the Eucharist*.
Has Sunday ever been a day of healing for me?

A PRAYER *for* MYSELF *when* VISITED *by* ANGER

Lord my God,
it has happened again and anger is visiting me.
I hear also your gospel call to love enemies,
to pray for persecutors, and to forgive.
Trusting in your way I pray:
I am angry right now with myself.
Judging is your job alone
for you alone have all the data.
Like others, I am created in your image
and loved by you without limit.
But there seems to be something unhealed in me;
I know not what it is,
and others may not know either,
but you, Lord, you know:
and I believe that you want to heal it.
This I ask you to do.
Lay onto me your healing touch. Amen.

MY SONG *to* JESUS

Text: from John 15, Stephen J. Wolf, 2007, 2016, public domain
tribute to the priesthood of Charley Giacosa
Music: BUNESSAN 5554 D, Scots Gaelic melody
Popular melody for *Morning Has Broken*

As Ab-ba loves you, Jes-sus you love me
Tell-ing me to re-main in your love
In your com-mand to love one an-oth-er
As you have loved me, call-ing me friend.

You are the vine and we are your branch-es;
Let Ab-ba prune me so I bear fruit.
Your word re-mem-b'ring, lov-ing the oth-er
As you have loved me, call-ing me friend.

No great-er love has one than to lay down
One's ver-y life for e-ven a friend.
We you have cho-sen, lov-ing each oth-er
As you have loved me, call-ing me friend.

We have been with you from the be-gin-ning
To tes-ti-fy in Spir-it and truth
In word and ac-tion, lov-ing each oth-er
As you have loved us, call-ing us friends.

III
Invited By Jesus
Mark 3:3

3 **He said
to the man with the withered hand,
"Come up here before us."**

Saint Ignatius of Loyola suggests a way to pray with scripture, especially around gospel stories with action. This way, from his *Spiritual Exercises*, is to let the gospel account be as an outline, presuming that the gospel writers never tell us everything that happened. For example, was it sunny, cloudy or rainy? Hot, cold, dry, humid? Are there noises or silence? Is there any music or background noise or conversation? What is on the minds of the people in the story? Can we tell whether it is indoors or outdoors? What kind of mood are Jesus and the disciples in? Is there anything there to eat or drink? Is anyone hungry or thirsty? OK, sometimes we are told some of these things, but never everything. Saint Ignatius suggests that we familiarize ourselves enough with the outline given in the gospel account, taking seriously what is there, and then place our very self into the story as one of the actual characters.

When I pray this way, I usually try to be simply a bystander, part of the crowd. But Jesus almost always makes me play the part of Peter or whoever the other main character is. When praying this particular story, the Lord has so far let me rest in the curious attentive anticipation of the synagogue crowd.

Try Saint Ignatius' *exercise* sometime when you have thirty minutes or an hour. Give yourself over to the story, and let your imagination pray through all your senses: sight, sound, smell, touch, hearing, and even your intuition and imagination. Let the whole story unfold. Let the Father and the Son through the Holy Spirit speak through the sacred word to your inmost being.

Have you ever been invited to a party to which you did not want to go? Ever been called with no warning to stand in front of a public gathering? What is the man thinking and feeling?

I have sometimes prayed this passage where the man with the withered hand is new to the community and does not know anything about Jesus. He is very uncertain about responding to being called to front and center, literally to "get up to the middle."

Another time, the man has been away during all the early activity, and though he has heard about this healer, this is the first time he has seen him. He is hopeful that he can be healed, and would ask for it if given the opportunity. Another time the hand had been withered since birth. Still another time, the withering was from a recent accident.

Gospel meditation sometimes transposes me to a work of art. In the wonderfully irreverent Monty Python movie *Life of Brian*, a beggar is bouncing around Brian, asking for alms for the poor. Brian tells the beggar that there is nothing to keep him from working, so stop bothering people and go get a job.

The man says, "I used to have a job. I was a crippled beggar. And then this Jesus came by and cured me. Took away my livelihood, he did." The exasperated Brian finally gives the bouncing beggar a coin to get rid of him, and in mock gratitude, the beggar says, "Oh, half a shekel! Thank you very much!" to which Brian replies, "There's no pleasing some people." The beggar bounces off out loud, "that's the same thing that Jesus said!"

Some of us with something withered do not want to be healed. We have grown used to our infirmity, thank you very much, and do not want any kind of change.

There is a difference between seeking a cure and learning to cope. I cannot be cured of the fact that I will someday die, so I learn to cope with it. If dying is our universal fear, it is the root of all other fears. We humans have tried all kinds of coping mechanisms:

denial; making the best of things; *eat and drink and enjoy the fruit of all (our) labor* (Ecclesiastes 3:13); ancestor worship; trying to live forever by amassing enough power, wealth, or the perfect diet or exercise to build what Ted Peters called a *citadel of psychic safety;* or trying to live as on an island in what another Lutheran Paul Tillich called *self-complacent finitude* (two country music songs just begging to be written). And there will always be people around, themselves in denial, to help us stay distracted in "methods" that offer no cure but plenty of pretense and coping.

As a Christian I want to argue that on Easter Sunday Christ did overcome death and so we have the cure to all our fear. Alas, we are still human. As a parishioner once put it so well, "I'm not afraid of death; I'm afraid of the dying, you know, the pain." When I quote Daffy Duck, "I don't like pain; it hurts me; I'm not like other people," I am most certainly using humor as my favorite coping mechanism.

So the man with the withered hand was invited to stand front and center, to bring his most urgent need for healing to Jesus. *So what (!)* if Jesus wants to make a point broader than that he has power to heal. *So what (!)* if the man is being used by Jesus as a visual aid to teach something to these scribes. *So what (!)* if the work that Jesus wants to accomplish in me is never only about or for me alone.

Once while praying this story I was on the edge of the crowd into which Jesus disappeared. He popped up behind me and pulled me into the field of grain to laugh in private about how the pharisees had acted, but was also sad that they could not give themselves permission to see the good things that God wanted to do in their lives. Still, he loved them.

Someday, I don't know when, I expect to pray this passage as the man with the withered hand. When I do, I expect to find out what it is that Christ wants to heal in me, the thing I don't even know is withered.

In the meantime, I can keep revisiting the way I feel blessed to name the core teachings of Jesus: love your enemies, pray for your persecutors, and forgive.

I invite you here to take a moment to reflect that most scholars think Mark was the earliest of the four canonical gospels to be written, probably in the mid '70's, forty years after the dying and rising of Jesus and not until the first witnesses to the Jesus story began to die. The early church was expecting Jesus to return soon, and we are still asked to watch ready.

Jesus is asking us to let him and the Father through their Holy Spirit breathe the grace into us to live now as people fully alive, as resurrected people, as if we were already in heaven. He knows we will fail often in this holy vocation. To this he calls us anyway, and he has shown us a way through failure.

Consider this Easter story toward the end of the gospel of John. The church is gathered in fear, in the upper room, behind doors locked tight. Afraid. Jesus breaks through their fear and the locked doors, and convinces them he is alive. (Was Mary offering intercessory prayer for them?) He then does something quite remarkable:

> Jesus **breathes** on them,
> saying,
>
> *Receive the holy Spirit.*
> *Whose sins you forgive*
> *are forgiven them,*
> *and whose sins you retain*
> *are retained.*
>
> John 20:22b,23

There is a context to the Upper Room story: we call it Good Friday. On the cross, Jesus would have been pulling himself up through the pain to take another breath. The decisive cause of death of most people who were crucified was suffocation, when they no longer had the strength to pull themselves up to breathe. In the second Genesis story of creation, God breathed the breath of life into Adam. We suffocated the Son, the New Adam, who then breathes the Holy Spirit, the Holy Breath, onto us.

This Easter story is one of the sources of our sacrament of reconciliation, indeed. It speaks also a truth for all people, one by one. We are set free. We may choose to hold onto the unforgiven, but to do so is to stay enslaved. We have been given by God the freedom, and by the Son the power, and by their Spirit the grace, to forgive. Embrace your humanity; hear the divine word of Christ within you; breathe in the Holy Spirit who has come to you. Accept the healing that will let you throw out coping. Breathe. Breathe deeply the freedom and power given you by our God.

+

**In the name of the Father
and of the Son
and of the Holy Breath of God.**

**Lord Jesus, Son of God and Son of Mary,
pattern of my life,
promise and image of who I am called to be,
help me to know and hold my anger
with grief that may turn it to compassion.**

**Risen Lord, with our Father,
keep breathing your Holy Spirit
over and into me
and to all who would be enemies
the desire and the power to forgive.**

Thanks be to you, God of the universe. Amen.

SOME QUESTIONS *for* PONDERING

1. Has Jesus invited me into his life and ministry as a bystander? A disciple? An apostle? A brother or sister?

2. What would it mean to ponder anger as a withered appendage?

3. A suggestion: Write on a piece of paper the most bothersome (to you) thing of creation; stretching to hold this honest scroll over a trash can, crumple the sheet into a ball, and let it fall, with a newly healthy high-five in the air.

   The satisfying symphony of a shredder-chew can also be a most healing noise. What else?

4. Perhaps Jesus' words to the man sound more as a command than an invitation. Which might better provoke in me the response Jesus seeks?

5. What is the difference between learning to cope and seeking a cure? Any examples in my story?

6. When in heaven, we will have let go of all in us that is unforgiven. How is Jesus calling me to be more alive in that way now?

7. Compare Jesus calling the man *into the middle* for teaching and healing with Jesus on the cross *in the middle* of two unnamed others.

ST. BENEDICT'S TWELVE STEPS *to* HUMILITY

1. Knowing that God sees me always, let me live in love with Jesus Christ, free from fear.

2. Seeking my deepest, most real desire, let me follow Christ, who followed the will of the Father.

3. Learning that I do not have every answer and that there are limits to what I can do, let me seek sources of help and guidance.

4. Admitting that every worthy commitment in life involves sacrifice and some difficulty, let me endure troubles in joyful fidelity.

5. Trusting that God's mercy is endless, though not my days on earth, let me honestly confess my sins.

6. Agreeing that all work has dignity, even the crude and harsh task, let me be content in my calling.

7. Accepting that for all the gifts and talents given me by God there will always be someone more wise, strong and beautiful, let me see myself as God sees me.

8. Seeing that I do not always have to win or get my way or be the one who is right, let me obey the rules of road and life which have been formed in community.

9. Believing that to judge is the job of God alone, let me withhold criticism and unsolicited advice.

10. Having seen misfortune laughed at and aware of my participation in the hurt, let me use humor only to give life.

11. Remembering past struggles to stay awake while others speak, and the annoying love of hearing my own voice, let me use as few words as possible.

12. Grateful to Jesus Christ who while fully divine humbled himself as fully human, even humbling himself on the cross, let me serve in humble confidence.

OUR SONG *to* JESUS

Text: from John 15, Stephen J. Wolf, 2007, 2016, public domain
tribute to the priesthood of Charley Giacosa
Music: BUNESSAN 5554 D, Scots Gaelic melody
Popular melody for ***Morning Has Broken***

As Ab-ba loves you, Je-sus you love us
Tell-ing us to re-main in your love
In your com-mand to love one an-oth-er
As you have loved us, call-ing us friends.

You are the vine and we are your branch-es;
Let Ab-ba prune us so we bear fruit.
Your word re-mem-b'ring, lov-ing each oth-er
As you have loved us, call-ing us friends.

No great-er love has one than to lay down
One's ver-y life for e-ven a friend.
We you have cho-sen, lov-ing each other
As you have loved us, call-ing us friends.

We have been with you from the be-gin-ning;
To tes-ti-fy in Spir-it and truth
In word and ac-tion, lov-ing each oth-er
As you have loved us, call-ing us friends.

IV
Riddle Silence
Mark 3:4

4 **Then he said to them,
"Is it lawful to do good on the sabbath
rather than to do evil,
to save life rather than destroy it?"
But they remained silent.**

I don't like to play games. I suppose it is because games with my seven brothers almost always broke up in fights. One by one every board game, electric football, mechanical basketball, every toy that involved a game disappeared mysteriously. I can't ask her now until heaven, but I'm pretty sure Momma confiscated them, like an efficient warden. There is a distant memory of her so much as admitting to one instance. Of course, this was for our own good, to help us live in peace. We invented our own. *Balloonsketball*, for example, was played with a balloon and a wire clothes hanger, bent into a hoop and hung over a door. It was a game you could play in silence when grounded.

So I don't like to play games. And I don't like riddles. Jesus, my Lord and Savior, likes riddles. And so I sometimes pray with his riddles.

They, the pharisees who are also in the synagogue, well, it seems that they do not like riddles either. My suspicion is that their teachers in pharisee school used riddles as part of their technique, and that they enjoyed it as much as I enjoyed teachers who used the so-called socratic method of debate teaching, which was not at all. Introverts consider it torture.

And so they remained silent. They gave Jesus the stone face. I know how to do that. I give it to the parishioner who is lambasting me about something, or the visitor who wishes to tell me in subtext that he or she is more holy than anyone in our parish, or the speaker who talks out of assumptions he or she thinks no one would dare to challenge as unorthodox. The stone face is a coping mechanism that helps me to keep an inner explosion from tipping into a tantrum of temper. The stone face is also a defensive power ploy, an attempt to say to the source of the inner boiling that, "you know, you really do not have this power you think you have over me." The stone face does not always work. Sometimes temper wins.

I suspect that the pharisees were using the tactic of the stone face. Is there any other reason for their silence? History might have something to tell us in the *Letter of the Pharisee*, a work of biblical imagination discovered in a box of old seminary homework:

Brothers and sisters in Christ,

When you asked me some weeks ago about my life as a pharisee, I thought it best to reflect on how best to explain this former identity. The Greek word pharisaioi *seems to be based on the Aramaic* perisaye *and the Hebrew* perusim, *which means the separated ones. We are not sure about its source, but it likely came from some of our detractors. We accepted being labeled as the separated ones because we saw it as our role to be an example, to be separated from those who are not yet following the law, the Torah. You see, we were good Jews, devout and pious. We were not ordained or anointed, but were recognized for our piety and our serious study.*

Our roots may have been in the 'scribes' of the law. We were learned, and emphasized knowledge and a strict interpretation of the Torah. This separated us, making us different from most of our kinsfolk who could not read or write. But we were not separated in our common goal: to be a holy nation, sacred and dedicated to THE LORD. *While the priests served God in the Jerusalem Temple, we were called to serve in our way of life. Our prayer was not limited to the temple sacrifice, but we were aware of what the priests did there. We watched the sacrifices to help make sure that ritual purity was maintained.*

Though all of the law given in the Torah was indispensable, we came to be marked as very strictly observing the sabbath, ritual purity regulations, and tithing. We made no apologies about this. We were proud of these observances as part of our Judean ancestry. We often had great influence in political and social matters, though some of our number may have involved themselves too much in such things.

Most of our focus was pointing out violations of the law. We were accused by some of writing our own laws, of doing what should only be done by THE LORD. *It was true that we relied on oral tradition as well as the written Torah, but that was to help people avoid breaching the Torah. Let me explain.*

In the normal course of life, a faithful Jew may set out to obey the Torah, living each moment completely aware of its 613 precepts. The laws might not be clear to a devoted but unsophisticated Jew, who would therefore benefit from a system of rituals of life.

Our rituals were meant to include the Torah plus other helpful ways to obey the Torah. They could be seen as a kind of fence around the law. The fence helped give people assurance of being faithful to the Torah itself. We felt we were serving the people by giving example and guidance in a way of life accessible to all, resulting in obedience to the Torah. There can be no question that the sabbath was observed more faithfully due to our influence.

We also dealt with the critical question of the Messiah; we waited with all of Judea. We pharisees considered it our duty to look for him with vigilance. The prophets told us he would be a descendant of David (Isaiah 11:2-5). We expected he would be the royal Savior, the one who would restore Israel to power. Until the Messiah came, we accepted it as the will of THE LORD *that we remain under Roman rule. Our role was to help find the Messiah and to make him known to the people. We also rooted out false messiahs, and there were many of them. We were confident that when the Messiah came, we would recognize him. As you know, in this almost all of us failed.*

And they remained silent. What if they had not remained silent? What if they had engaged Jesus in some gutsy back and forth? Imagine that they find the freedom-courage to dance in the Jesus' riddle, that they slowly come to realize there is nothing to fear in Jesus except the fear of letting go of being afraid.

Imagine they slowly appreciate sharing in their common vocabulary: the Hebrew Scriptures! They poke each other with the holy word from morning to dark. The crowd becomes entertained, and both Jesus and the pharisees become energized. They come to see the wisdom connected to the love they begin to sense starting to leak out of each other, love leaking out all over the place…

Alas, that is not how things played out; and it can be distressing to see things still not playing out the way Jesus would prefer. Worse yet, there are people who think that forgiveness is an impossible and self-defeating waste of energy. We beg to differ, for we do see miracles happen around forgiveness. And there is evidence to encourage us. One example is something called the *Enright Forgiveness Process Model*. I have used this model, found in *Men and Abortion* by Catherine Coyle, for folks working through the pain of the aftermath of abortion. A critical piece of this model is something called REFRAMING, which in Christian terms will mean the grace of being open to see the other a bit more as he or she is seen by God.

The whole model begins with examination of any denial or coping mechanisms used, awareness of anger, admitting any appropriate shame, asking how something in my story still has a hook on me, whether I keep repeating "cognitive rehearsal" of an event, discerning whether there has in fact been a permanent change, along with issues of justice, right and wrong. A decision to forgive can begin with openness to a change of heart or new insights to how old ways are not working, and considering forgiveness as a viable option. Reframing means to view myself or the other in as large a context as possible, seeking the empathy that comes with understanding, feeling compassion in suffering with the other, even absorbing the pain. Then meaning can be found in remembering that I have needed others' forgiveness in the past, the truth that I am not alone, realizing that I may have a new purpose in life, and the miracle of emotional release:

A FORGIVENESS MODEL

1. Accepting God's complete love.
2. Practicing awareness of self and feelings and emotions and all of created reality.
3. Prayerful reflection on the communion of saints, all of whom no longer hold anything unforgiven.
4. Admitting the objective truth of any injustice done *to* me.
5. Confession of the immorality of any injustice done *by* me.
6. Sitting with God in feelings from grief, especially anger, sadness, fear, loneliness, shame, pride…
7. With neither condemnation nor complacency, honest appraisal of culpability, the extent to which I have acted without freedom, or the possibility that others may have.
8. Asking for the charity to see myself and all involved with God's eyes of love, compassion and mercy.
9. Sitting for a while in the middle of the delight God takes in one enemy praying for another.
10. Being open to however the Holy Spirit prompts me toward some kind of healing act of charity.

SOME QUESTIONS *for* PONDERING

1. Can I name a way of thinking in the Church or in my culture that I used to find helpful but now see with wider eyes?

2. If I were a pharisee or a scribe in the Judean first century AD, how might I have responded to the riddle of Jesus?

3. An old friend asked how to give the *stone face* over the phone. How would I answer this question?

4. Silence can be a way to listen.
   Silence can be a power play.
   Silence can be a sitting in fear.
   Silence can be . . . ?

5. *You could not be in conflict with another person, if so to speak what you dislike in him were not in you... The reason we are always looking for faults in other people is because of faults in ourselves. There is a rebel in us that we refuse to accept. In proportion that we do, we can accept others.*   - Thomas Merton

   What would the pharisees and Jesus have been able to recognize in each other?

6. Has new data about a person or situation ever made forgiving or asking forgiveness possible?

7. One brother will finish an anger-showing with:
   ...and why am I yelling!?!,
   and then imitate a comic's imitation of Robin Leach on "Lifestyles of the Rich and Famous":
   I'm talking loud! I don't know why!

   Does humor more often help me to REFRAME a situation or to hide from the emotion of anger?

A PRAYER *for an* INSTITUTION

Lord my God,
it has happened again and anger is visiting me.
I hear also your gospel call to love enemies,
to pray for persecutors, and to forgive.
Because I trust in your way I pray:
I am angry right now with _____.
name of institution

This institution is made up of human beings
who like me are created in your image
and are loved by you without limit.
But it seems to be a sick institution,
and its people seem not to know they are in
a sick institution; but you, Lord, you know:
and I believe that you want to heal
every broken structure in every human society.
Lay your healing touch into the center of this
institution and give its people the free courage
to seek the healing you want to give. Amen.

EZEKIEL SONG

Text: Ezekiel 36:24-28, Stephen J. Wolf, 2013, 2016, public domain
Music: 888, O FILII ET FILIAE, Chant Mode II, Airs sur les hymnes sacrez, 1623
Popular melody for *Ye Sons and Daugh-\ters Let-\ Us Sing*

REFRAIN: **Y**ou are our God\,
                 your peo-ple are we, A-le-lu-ia!

Lord God/, Sab-a-oth, El, A-do-nai,
Proph-et E-ze-ki-el's song we lift high:
Spir-it and heart\, re-newed you pro-vide,
You are our God...

                                               REFRAIN

Take us out-side of our pride that div-ides,
Gath-er us in from all na\-tions wide,
Bring us back in-to your land at your side,
You are our God...

                                               REFRAIN

Sprin-kle on-to us your wa\-ters clean,
From our im-pur-it-ies help us to wean,
Clean from i-dol-a-try let us be seen,
You are our God...

                                               REFRAIN

Take from our flesh\ these hearts\ of stone,
Make in us new hearts of flesh\ not bone,
In-side our be-ing your Spir-it be shown,
You are our God...

                                               REFRAIN

V
Anger-Grief
Mark 3:5

**5   Looking around at them with anger
and grieved at their hardness of heart,
he said to the man,
"Stretch out your hand."
He stretched it out
and his hand was restored.**

So, here's the word. **Anger**. The gospel of Mark tells us that Jesus was angry.

Having hung in this long, you may have gone to your dictionary by now. Let's take a look.

These are from an old *Webster's New World Dictionary* in a Trappist monastery guest house library:

an.ger (ang'ger), *n.* a feeling of being very annoyed and wanting to fight back at a person or thing that hurts one or is against one; wrath; rage.

grief (gref), *n.* 1. deep and painful sorrow, as that caused by someone's death. 2. something that causes such sorrow. **-come to grief**, to fail or be ruined.

Anger is an emotion. Say it out loud: *Anger is an emotion*. It is not imaginary; it is real. It is like hunger and thirst: anger is part of our human nature. Like hunger and thirst, anger is a feeling that first comes to us, arrives at the scene, almost always as a surprise visitor. Free will enters when we choose what we *do* with it. But before we can *choose* what to do with it, we have to become *aware* that the emotion of anger is upon us. Am I able to recognize an arrival of anger?

I think that Jesus is showing us through this story how the process of *awareness* then *choice* can unfold.

Like you and me, Jesus is a human being, fully human. Fully human and fully divine. Fully God and fully man. As a teacher Eugene LaVerdiere liked to put it, "not God on his Poppa's side and human on his Momma's side," understood by some incorrectly as half God and half man. No, we proclaim Jesus as fully God and fully human. OK, the Church argued quite a bit and quite vehemently before we came to a consensus about how best to speak of the two natures of Christ. The result uses 20 of the 32 lines that make up the Nicene Creed, formulated for the most part at the Council of Nicea in 325 A.D.

The Greek word used in Mark 3:5, **orge** (pronounced or-gae'), could probably be translated as *wrath* instead of *anger*. We tend to think of *wrath* as a word to use for the divine, as in *the wrath of God*. If the gospel writer is pointing to the humanity of Jesus, we can see it in the use of the word *anger*, and in the very telling of this story of Jesus failing.

Remember, the gospel of Mark was written in perhaps around 75 A.D. for a community undergoing persecution, and so dealing with their own difficulties. Mark has been called *a passion narrative with a prologue*. An unexpected failure can be a powerful prompter of the anger emotion. Perhaps Jesus is angry about his own inability to break through to the pharisees, to win them over so they can see his side of the story.

Every preacher wants converts. Few experiences give me as much simple selfish joy as when a fellow Christian who still agrees with using the death penalty steps up after mass to report, even as one retired police officer once put it with his forefinger and thumb almost touching in the air between us, "Father, you *almost* had me that time." This was big.

My suspicion is that the source of the emotion of anger in our story is the silence of the pharisees. They will not even talk to him. They will talk *about* him, but they refuse to enter into dialogue with Jesus. And this makes him hopping mad.

There are two reasons that I suggest Mark 3:1-6 as a penance in the sacrament of reconciliation when a person expresses the desire to be healed of anger. The first reason is the gospel truth that in his humanity Jesus too was angry. The second reason is what he does in this story with his anger. He grieves.

His grief is over their hardness of heart. The root of the Greek word for *hardness* is **porow**, or *poroo*, pronounced *po-ro'o*, apparently from **poros**, (a kind of stone); to *petrify*, that is, (figuratively) to *indurate* (*render stupid* or *callous*): -blind, harden.

Their hearts, made by God to be beating, living, had become in them petrified, like stone, by their own choice it seems. They have already been losing these battles of wits with Jesus, so it is easier to give a stubborn stone face that reflects the hard heart. They won't lose if they refuse to play the game.

We are not told what it is that Jesus sees in their hearts. We were told four episodes earlier, in the event with the paralytic, that Jesus *knew in his mind what they were thinking to themselves*. How frightened must they have become when they heard Jesus say out loud, *why are you thinking such things in your hearts?* (2:8). Perhaps this is why they remained silent when faced with his riddle, scared to tangle with one who knows their own thoughts and feelings. Is that a fair fight?

Here we are faced with the difference between Jesus and me. OK, there are **many** ways that I am unlike Jesus; OK, admitted. So here is one difference between Jesus and me: I can never really know what is going on in the heart of another human being. How sadly unaware can I be of how my own heart moves! This is why to judge is the job of God alone, who searches the mind and knows the heart (Psalms 7:10b, 94:11, and all of Psalm 139). We humans lack the insight to judge each other well. Jesus can look into the human heart and see desires, motivations, imperfections, and blockages. Like an X-ray that can see a blocked artery, Jesus can see a stone wall erected in a heart. So why doesn't he just break down that wall, explode those stumbling blocks? An answer is in how God created us with freedom. Freedom means that we can choose to love God, and that we can choose to not love God. Freedom matters; we are not robots. When we love God, it matters that we do so freely and not as slaves. But God compels us to enter this freedom.

Here we have a big-time paradox. The saints define freedom as the capacity to say only yes to God. When I say this to young adults, they give me the turned-head look that a young dog gives when you make a strange noise, or they stare defiantly at the man (me) whose sanity they now question. If sanity is what generates the world's way of dealing with anger, perhaps we are all in need of a little gospel craziness.

The saints are getting at this: As long as I am unable to say *yes* to God, then I am still somehow enslaved to something other than God. I am not yet free.

Saintly freedom, then, is not the blessing of many options, but the grace to know which of them is the one God desires that I choose. As the Trappist monk Thomas Merton put it, when I am in touch with God's deepest desire for me then I am in touch with my deepest and most real desire for myself. To be able to choose accordingly is to be free.

These pharisees are not free. The stone wall in their hearts reflected in the stone wall on their faces might have been built by them of their own free will. Who in that synagogue could know the desires, motivations, imperfections and blockages of those pharisees? God alone. Jesus, in his divinity, sees all of it, even the blockages to which they are blind. He wants to heal them. But God will not violate our freedom. In his divinity, Jesus will not force his healing on them, and in his humanity he fails to cajole them into freedom. For some reason, they will not enter into dialogue with him. Anger rises within our Lord, and he turns to them.

What does he then do with his anger? He is grieved. He holds the emotion of anger with grief. He holds the humanity of his anger in his divine hand of compassion. He does the same thing that is so often the only thing God can do with us: compassion. He *suffers with*.

And that man with the withered hand? Jesus asks him to do what the pharisees were unwilling or unfree to do, to **stretch**.

Commenting on the promise in the First Letter of John, that we will see God as God is, Saint Augustine calls us to be busy about desiring this vision of God: *The entire life of a good Christian is in fact an exercise of holy desire... By stretching (a wineskin) you increase the capacity of the sack, and this is how God deals with us. Simply by making us wait God increases our desire, which in turn enlarges the capacity of our soul, making it able to receive what is to be given us.*

The Church teaches that this *desire for God is written in the human heart, because humans are created by God and for God; and God never ceases to draw us to God.*

We are created with a capacity for God, but this capacity can dissipate when we hide behind the stone wall. The man's silent stretch is an obedience without assurance or even warning about what will happen.

The man does stretch out his hand, a gesture like Mary's *fiat*, her *yes*, and he is made whole, restored to the way he was created in God's image. He can throw away his coping skills, because he is cured.

A reader asked if I have more to say about **grief**. This book has really been about anger, and less about grief. I often call myself a very slow griever. Not a problem; we all do it differently. Unique grieving is wrapped up in the unique way each of us is made in God's image. And true grief is almost always a sign that what is lost is love. If the five steps of grief are on target (*denial; anger; bargaining; depression; acceptance*), anger is for me the hardest part. So let's be easy on each other with how we grieve, and put this too in the strong hands of the Lord. Let true grief give honor to the love wrapped up in what we have lost.

One of my favorite sayings about grief touches the core of healing to be found in forgiveness. It is from graphic truth-telling of a man who was abused as a teen, who discovered what I recognize as sanity in a friend's response, "that's tricky" to his all-of-a-sudden declaration:

> *It's letting go of the sense that the past
> should have been any different or better.*
>
> Martin Moran,
The Tricky Part

Mr. Moran's inspiration is often the best I know to offer, except for the word of God to which I tether my soul on days of depression. These words too I offer, which can be found in your Bible or in two of my little prayer books. *In Health & In Healing* is from a short hospital chaplaincy where I watched faithful Baptists, Methodists, and others eat the word the way Catholics take in Holy Communion. *31 Days of God's Love-Call* is a Hebrew scripture passage for each day of a month.

IN HEALTH & IN HEALING

Sunday	am	Psalm 100	Mark 16:5-6
	pm	Psalm 23	1 Corinthians 15:3-8
Monday	am	Psalm 42:1-6a	Matthew 8:1-3
	pm	Psalm 121	Ezekiel 36:24-28
Tuesday	am	Psalm 139:1-10	Mark 3:1-5
	pm	Psalm 84:1-9	Ephesians 2:19-22
Wednesday	am	Psalm 63:1-8	Romans 8:22-27
	pm	Psalm 131	Philippians 2:5-11
Thursday	am	Psalm 86:1-7,11	Romans 8:14-17
	pm	Psalm 126	Luke 6:17-19
Friday	am	Psalm 51:10-19	Luke 17:20-21
	pm	Psalm 65:4,9-13	John 14:1-7
Saturday	am	Psalm 46	Ephesians 3:16-22
	pm	Psalm 147:1-11	Matthew 8:23-27

31 DAYS of GOD's LOVE-CALL

1 Psalm 63:1-8　**2** Psalm 46　**3** Isaiah 55:1-13
4 Wisdom of Solomon 9:1-6,9-11　**5** Psalm 23
6 Psalm 139:1-18,23-24　**7** Isaiah 43:1-5a　**8** Exodus 16:4-5,9,10b
9 Hosea 2:10-22　**10** Psalm 131　**11** Psalm 8　**12** Psalm 103
13 Psalm 104　**14** Psalm 19　**15** 1st Kings 19:4-9a,11-13
16 Jeremiah 29:11-14　**17** Ezekiel 16:4-13　**18** Jeremiah 18:1-6
19 Genesis 2:4-25　**20** Genesis 1:24-31　**21** Isaiah 54:4-10
22 Deuteronomy 30:15-20　**23** Isaiah 62:1-5
24 Ecclesiastes 3:1-11,14b　**25** Psalm 62:2-10,12,13a
26 Wisdom of Solomon 11:21-12:1　**27** Psalm 91:1-12,14-16
28 Ezekiel 36:24-28　**29** Ezekiel 37:1-14
30 Isaiah 40:1-11　**31** Psalm 130

Some of the readings are in both collections.
Feel free to copy this page to keep in your Bible.

SOME QUESTIONS *for* PONDERING

1. How would I describe anger to a ten-year-old?

2. *The scars left from the child's defeat in the fight against irrational authority are at the bottom of every neurosis.* — Erich Fromm

   Is this why Jesus welcomed children?

3. In what way or ways has my anger come from failure or powerlessness?

4. *Denial. Anger. Bargaining. Depression. Acceptance.*
   (Kubler-Ross' five stages of grief)

   Is anger simply a natural human part of the growth we call conversion?

5. *The anger, which has in it no element of personal rancor, is such as may justly be felt at the spectacle of people whose fidelity to the Law is matched by blindness to moral values.* — Vincent Taylor

   To what might Jesus want to open my eyes?

6. *Matthew and Luke omit mention of the anger of Christ, perhaps consciously avoiding the attribution of any shortcoming to him. But the passion is a human one and its exercise in the face of cultivated blindness of spirit is no sin. Mark is therefore the better witness to the incarnation.* — Gerard S. Sloyan

   What makes us uncomfortable about Jesus being angry?

7. What do I think about one sister's statement
that all any of us want to do
is make a meaningful contribution?

8. Am I still waiting for Jesus to call me to stretch?

A PRAYER *for* MORE EXPERIMENTING

Lord my God,
it has happened again and anger is visiting me.
I still hear your gospel call to love enemies,
to pray for persecutors, and to forgive.
Trusting in your way I pray:
I am still angry with *N*.
Judging is your job alone
for you alone have all the data.
Like me, *N*. is created in your image
and loved by you without limit.
But there seems to be something unhealed in *N*.;
I know not what it is,
and *N*. may not know either,
but you, Lord, you know:
and I believe that you want to heal it.
This I ask you to do.
Lay onto *N*. your healing touch.
Amen.

ANOTHER SONG *from* JESUS

Text: from John 15, Stephen J. Wolf, 2007, 2016, public domain
tribute to the priesthood of Charley Giacosa
Music: BUNESSAN 5554 D, Scots Gaelic melody
Popular melody for *Morning Has Broken*

As Ab-ba loves me so do I love you.
I tell you this: re-main in my love.
Keep this com-mand-ment: Love one an-oth-er
As I have loved you, call-ing you friend.

I am the vine and you are my branch-es;
Let Ab-ba prune you so you bear fruit.
As I have loved you, love one an-oth-er.
My word re-mem-ber: you are my friend.

No great-er love has one than to lay down
One's ver-y life for e-ven a friend.
As I have loved you, love one an-oth-er;
You I have cho-sen, call-ing you friend.

You have been with me from the be-gin-ning;
Tes-ti-fy in the Spir-it of truth.
In word and ac-tion: Love one an-oth-er
As I have loved you, call-ing you friend.

VI
Turning to Freedom
Mark 3:6

**6 The Pharisees went out
and immediately
took counsel with the Herodians
against him to put him to death.**

We are told how this complicated story ends. These pharisees, toward whom Jesus feels both anger and grief, awareness and compassion: they go out to make plans with people who know Herod how best to kill Jesus. His choice is compassion. Theirs is violence plotted with bitter enemies in the intramural fight for the heart and soul of their people.

Does this make you sad? It makes me sad. Not depressed, just sad. When I look upon or paint an image of Christ on the cross, I know as I have known since the Sisters of Mercy did their thing for me at Saint Ann School that he died for **my** sins.

In my one summer as a hospital chaplain, I got to know a delightful man who grew up as a Jew in a Catholic neighborhood. The kids beat him up, stole his lunch, and said ugly things to him about Jews. He had become convinced that we named as *Judas* the one who betrayed Jesus because *Judas* sounds like *Jew*.

I apologized to him, but he did not want my apologies. He was given pause when I told him that whenever I have heard the name *Judas*, what enters my mind is that Judas represents me, because Jesus died for my sins. It had never occurred to me how a Jewish kid in a Catholic neighborhood might hear the name *Judas* in a different way. I still feel the bond of compassion that I felt that day with him.

What can I do when I am angry with even my brother? This is not theoretical for me. Some years ago God graced me with a way to pray this. With the gift of imagination, I stand next to the brother, with him in front of our God, and I pray something like:

Loving Abba, this is my brother,
and you know my feelings and our entire story.
Lord, I believe that as you created me in your image,
so too you created my brother in your image.
Lord, created in your image? Hard time seeing it!
But you alone see everything in both of our hearts.
Lord, I don't want to see everything you see,
because I am not yet ready for it all;   John 16:12
but could you show me something today
of how my brother and I are both created in your image?
Help me to feel my anger with grief and compassion,
knowing as did your Son whom they wanted to kill
that we are all broken, wounded in our humanity.

Another religious practice, if I may be a pharisee, is to offer intercessory prayer for myself and the person with whom I am angry. These gifts make this possible:

1. faith in God's love for all people,
2. the truth that it is not possible for me to know everything going on in the heart of another person,
3. the likelihood that God alone knows what is blocking the person with whom I am angry from being open to reconciliation or health, and (*gulp*)
4. even the grace of accepting that the real problem may be me and not the other.

Anger is righteous only when I am in the right. Truly, how often am I completely just and righteous? Don't answer that. Almost* always I am responsible at least partially for what has gone wrong whether by trying to control a person or a situation or by having unrealistic expectations. (*I say *almost always* because of exceptions, such as any kind of child abuse, when the adult is always the one responsible.) But even a truly innocent victim will eventually need the healing of the emotion of anger that comes only in forgiving.

When graced with the gift of awareness that the one with whom I am angry is, like me, created in God's own image, adopted as God's own daughter or son, then I might be ready for intercessory prayer. One way to ponder intercessory prayer is as a way to give God permission to do what God already wants to do.

I am not talking out of both sides of my mouth. If I am in an unhealthy place in my life, I might not be free or capable of asking God for the help I need, and which I desire without even knowing it. I might be so angry with God as to ask God to just leave me alone. God respects my freedom. However, if my friend, **or my enemy**, asks God to intercede, to make the healing touch that God already wants to make, then God can respect the freedom of my friend **or of my enemy**, and then freely heal me.

The Church teaches with wisdom that each passage of sacred scripture is best read in the context of **all** of scripture. As you think of our story of the anger-grief of Jesus, what other passages of the Bible or words from our faith tradition come to mind? Here are some to which I am drawn:

You have heard that it was said to your ancestors, 'You shall not kill...' But I say to you, don't stay angry with your brother or call him *raqa* (an imbecile or a blockhead) (Mt 5:21-22). The theologian and author of Ephesians adds: *Be angry but do not sin; do not let the sun set on your anger* (Ephesians 4:26). I find as helpful supports to this teaching two images from the Wisdom Book of Sirach: *Wrath and anger are hateful things, yet the sinner hugs them tight* (Sirach 27:30), and *If you blow upon a spark, it quickens into flame, if you spit on it, it dies out; yet both you do with your mouth* (Sirach 28:12). Notice in our story that **Jesus turns**. In Jesus' turning there is time. The time it takes for him to turn is time enough for his anger to be overcome with healing grief.

Let me say it this way: He lets his human anger be overwhelmed by divine compassion. Jesus gives himself a little time for this. So often, my choice is to feed the anger with fertilizing words and raging water and burning sun, to do whatever it takes to keep the spark of anger alive, even to the point of pleasure. Jesus shows us a different way.

Go first and be reconciled with your brother, and then come and offer your gift at the altar (Mt 5:24). Jesus calls us to make peace. Few of us want this job. We have it anyway.

You have heard that it was said, 'You shall love your neighbor and hate your enemy (see Leviticus 19:18), *but I say to you, love your enemies, and pray for those who persecute you, that you may be children of your heavenly Father, for he makes his sun rise on the bad and the good, and causes rain to fall on the just and the unjust* (Mt 5:43-45). An old friend still says this is the most difficult of all of the teachings of Jesus. I cannot do it on my own. I cannot do it without God's grace, but I can ask God for that grace.

Words of scripture we know as the Lord's Prayer say so much of what Jesus has taught us:

...And forgive us...as we forgive... (Mt 6:12)

How much of our lives do we spend trying to find another way? This **is** the way.

St. Paul's excellent teaching is also a huge help: *If your enemy is hungry, feed him* (Romans 12:20). Paul's practical advice is as effective as it is difficult.

And the theologian Saint Pope John Paul II, after the September 11, 2001 attack, said to the world: *No peace without justice... no justice without forgiveness...*, building on Pope Paul VI's often quoted maxim: *If you want peace, work for justice.* Adding *forgiveness* to Paul VI's maxim, John Paul II spoke an essential truth. One of my teachers in the Holy Land was a priest who had spent the bulk of his adult life as a counselor to teenagers, but who was then a peace worker for the United Nations. He said there would not be peace in the Middle East until someone with enough courage willingly ends the cycle of retaliation by forgiving. It hit me one day, listening to him, how central is forgiveness to the Christian identity.

At the sacrament of Baptism, the one made newly wet *in the name of the Father and of the Son and of the Holy Spirit* (Mt 28:19) is "anointed" (which is what the word *Christ* means) with oil, and then given this message of our vocation:

> **As Jesus Christ was anointed**
> **priest, prophet and king,**
> **so may you live always**
> **as a member of his body...**

As a **prophet**, the Christian will be called to proclaim a truth to somebody who God wants to hear that truth, and to speak that truth with compassion. As a **king or queen**, the Christian will be called to use his or her gifts, abilities, strengths and *charisms* in service of humanity, sometimes as leader, always as a servant. As a **priest**, the Christian will be called to pray and forgive. We cannot wriggle out of our vocation of forgiveness. When the apostles were bluntly told of their vocation to forgive, not seven or seventy times but seven times seventy times, their response was from the gut: ***Increase our faith!*** (Luke 17:5)

We too ask our Lord and Savior (who entered human history as Son of God and Son of Man to dwell in our midst, share our experience, and show us the way; who gave himself completely in his teaching and preaching and healing ministry even to dying for us on the cross; who was raised from the dead, appeared to the women and the apostles and the disciples who recognized him in the breaking of the bread (Lk 24:31);

who having told Mary Magdalene to not cling to him, ascended to the Father and with the Father sent their Holy Spirit upon the Church beginning at Pentecost and continuing even to this very day) we too can ask for the grace we know we will need to forgive and to keep on forgiving, by echoing the apostles:

Lord, increase our faith!

These reflections are the fruit of years of Ignatian prayer with this anger story, sitting with strong emotions and feelings in the fear-free safety of the presence of the Risen Lord, and many graced encounters with people of faith. I invite you to find a quiet place, sit, breathe, and simply ask for the Lord's healing touch.

God wants to heal every core wound in the family of God's sons and daughters. We are free to accept that healing, and we are free to stay in our unhealedness. To heal us, Jesus has asked us to love our enemies, to pray for our persecutors, and to forgive. If I cannot yet love my enemy or forgive, I can nevertheless pray for my persecutor(s) as Jesus taught me, as Jesus did even on the cross: *Father, forgive them for they know not what they do* (Luke 23:34).

And if I cannot even do this, Lord, help me to *fake it 'til I make it*, by your grace, as you keep speaking your love into my inmost being:

My Beloved,

I have made you in my image,
one and unique,
not like anyone ever has been
or ever will be made in my image.
Having made you,
I know you,
all the great things
your ego wants everyone to know,
those things
you do not want anyone to know,
and everything
you do not yet know yourself.
And in knowing you,
I love you,
neither because of your strengths
nor in spite of your weaknesses;
there is nothing you can do
that will make me love you,
and there is nothing you can do
that will keep me from loving you.
Remember this always:
that I love you just is.

- **God**

SOME QUESTIONS FOR PONDERING

1. Immediately. Right away. The pharisees waste no time in making their plans. Are they angry too?

2. The five verses following this anger-grief story are highlighted in the New American Bible Revised Edition as *The Mercy of Jesus*. Mercy? Really? While they are making plans to kill him?

3. A hospice chaplain defined forgiveness as *the release of a toxic grudge*.
   If I were graced with the ability to choreograph a dance-turn of release for another, might I be able to dance it also for myself?

4. *God judged it better to bring good out of evil than to allow nothing evil to exist.*
   - Saint Augustine, *The Enchiridion*, #27

   Can any good come out of my anger story?

5. Intercessory prayer can be the riskiest of all prayer, for God's answer might include my doing of something I don't want. Risk. Do I desire freedom enough to take this risk?

6. *To love is to will the good of another.*
   Saint Thomas Aquinas, CCC 1766

   If this seems impossible, what else can be done?

TAKING ANGER *into* THE TRINITY

✝

**In the name of the Father
and of the Son
and of the Holy Breath of God.**

**Lord Jesus,
Son of God and son of Mary,
pattern of my life,
promise and image of who I am called to be,
help me to know and hold my anger
with grief that may turn it to compassion.**

**Risen Lord,
with our Father,
keep breathing your Holy Spirit
over and into me
and to all who would be enemies
the desire and the power
to forgive.**

**Form us into the Easter people
you created us to be.**

**Thanks be to you,
One God of all creation.**

Amen.

Sources and For More

Page 24: *...a feast fit for a king...*; Frederick Buechner, *Wishful Thinking: A Seeker's ABC*, Harper San Francisco, 1993, pg. 2.

Page 27: St. Ignatius of Loyola, d. 1556, *The Spiritual Exercises*, especially paragraphs 122-125. The best way to experience the exercises is on an individually directed retreat. Find Jesuit retreat centers at www.jesuits.org/retreat-centers.

Page 28: *...get up to the middle...*; Joanna Dewey, *Markan Public Debate*, Society of Biblical Literature, 1980, pg. 102.

Page 29: *Monty Python's Life of Brian*, 1979, 94 minutes, Brian is born on the original Christmas, in the stable next door. Rated R, not for children, No Way, much of the bad language is terribly unnecessary. The humor is masterful. My report is from weak memory; in the movie the man was a leper instead of a cripple:

Ex-Leper: Okay, sir, my final offer: half a shekel for an old ex-leper?
Brian: Did you say "ex-leper"?
Ex-Leper: That's right, sir, 16 years behind a veil and proud of it.
Brian: Well, what happened?
Ex-Leper: Oh, cured, sir.
Brian: Cured?
Ex-Leper: Yes sir, bloody miracle, sir. Bless you!
Brian: Who cured you?
Ex-Leper: Jesus did, sir. I was hopping along, minding my own business, all of a sudden, up he comes, cures me! One minute I'm a leper with a trade, next minute my livelihood's gone. Not so much as a by-your-leave! "You're cured, mate." Bloody do-gooder.
Brian: Well, why don't you go and tell him you want to be a leper again?

Ex-Leper: Uh, I could do that sir, yeah. Yeah, I could do that I suppose. What I was thinking was I was going to ask him if he could make me a bit lame in one leg during the middle of the week. You know, something beggable, but not leprosy, which is a pain in the...
Brian: There you are.
Ex-Leper: Half a dinare for me bloody life story?
Brian: There's no pleasing some people.
Ex-Leper: That's just what Jesus said, sir.

Page 30:...*citadel of psychic safety*...; Ted Peters, *Sin: Radical Evil in Soul & Society*, 1999.

Page 30:...*self-complacent finitude*...; Paul Tillich, *The Religious Situation*, 1925.

Page 35: *St. Benedict's Twelve Steps to Humility*; Saint Benedict of Nursia, d. 547, *The Rule*, drawn from Chapter 7, adapted from the 1975 Image Books translation by Anthony C. Meisel and M.L. del Mastro, previously used by the author in *God's Money* in 2009 and *40 Penances for Spiritual Exercise* in 2014.

Page 39:...*Brothers and Sisters*...; Steve Wolf, *Letter of the Pharisee*, from a homework assignment at Mundelein Seminary, offered with most sincere apologies to all.

Page 42: *The Enright Forgiveness Process Model*; Robert Enright, *Forgiveness Is a Choice*, Washington, D.C.: APA Books, 2001. For more, visit the International Forgiveness Institute web site at internationalforgiveness.com.

Page 42: *A Forgiveness Model*; generalized from the author's *Sons of Adam*, a prayer and companion workbook for the outstanding book by C.T. Boyle, Ph.D., *Men and Abortion: A Path to Healing*, Life Cycle Books, 1999.

Page 44: *You could not be in conflict...*; Thomas Merton, Tape 73-2, Gettsemani Abbey, Kentucky, transcribed by John Raub in 1975

Page 47: *anger, grief,* from *Webster's New World Dictionary.* Friend and scholar, James Pratt, S.J. is the first who told me that the phrase can also mean that his bowels turned inward, a way to also understand compassion.

Page 47: *...anger...; Mark 3:5* in some different translations:
...looking around at them with **anger** and grieved at their
hardness of heart... (*New American Bible*)
...when he had looked round about on them with **anger**,
being grieved for the hardness of their hearts... (*King James*)
...looking at them with **anger**, but sorrowing for their
obdurate stupidity... (*The Anchor Bible*)
...he looked around at them with **anger**, grieved at
their hardness of heart... (*Revised Standard Version*)
...He looked around at them with **anger**; he was grieved at
their hardness of heart... (*New Revised Standard Version*)
...looking round on them with **anger**,
being greatly grieved on the hardness of the heart of them...
(*Marshall's Interlinear Literal Translation*)
...And he looked at them with **anger**, sad because of the
hardness of their hearts... (*Holman, from the Peshitta*)

Page 48:...*God on his poppa's side...,* Eugene LaVerdierre. I was blessed to be a student of Gene, but must confess that this phrase often quoted by me is quoted by Bill Huebsch who put it this way in another favorite book, *A Spirituality of Wholeness: the New Look at Grace* , Mystic, Connecticut: Twenty-Third Publications, 1988:

We are not alone. And Jesus was not alone either. We often misunderstand this in the gospels. We think, Well, Jesus was God. He was all powerful. He didn't have to deal with life the way I do...

Jesus is God. No doubt about it. But he is also human, very human, completely human, humanly human.

He ate, drank, slept, urinated, sweated, wept, worried, sang, told stories, was aroused, worked, got blisters, made mistakes, and generally was a regular type of guy.

Jesus was human and he faced all that humans face. He wasn't half human and half divine, Gene LaVerdiere has pointed out, you know, sort of human on his mother's side and divine on his father's side!

No. He was fully human and fully divine. This is mysterious and hard to understand, but it is also very important.

Page 50: *hardness*, from *Strong's Concordance*.

Page 52: One example of this is in Thomas Merton, *Learning To Love, Journals, Volume 6*, Christine M. Bochen, Editor, San Francisco: HarperSanFrancisco, 1998, pg. 321:

One...work(s) at solitude, not by putting fences around oneself, but by destroying all fences and throwing away all the disguises, getting down to the naked core of one's inmost desire, which is the desire of liberty - reality...to be real in the freedom which reality gives when one is rightly related to it.

See also chapter 27, *What is Liberty?* in *New Seeds of Contemplation* by Thomas Merton, New York: New Directions Books, 1961, pp. 199-202.

Page 53: *The entire life of a good Christian...*, Saint Augustine, d.430, Tract 4: PL 35, 2008-2009, *Liturgy of the Hours*, Office of Readings, Friday, Week Six.

Page 53: *...desire for God...*; *Catechism of the Catholic Church*, United States Conference of Catholic Bishops, 1994, 1997, #27.

Page 54: Martin Moran, *The Tricky Part: A Boy's Story of Sexual Trespass, A Man's Journey to Forgiveness*, Beacon Press, 2005, Anchor Books, 2006. This is well written, graphic, profound, and funny. He tells the truth with compassion. For adults only.

Page 55: *In Health & In Healing* and *31 Days of God's Love-Call*; by Stephen Joseph Wolf, visit idjc.org.

Page 56: *The anger which has in it…*; Vincent Taylor, *The Gospel According to St. Mark*, Macmillon & Co. Ltd., 1953, pg. 223.

Page 56: *Matthew and Luke omit…*; Gerard S. Sloyan, "The Gospel of Saint Mark," *New Testament Reading Guide*, Collegeville, Minn.: The Liturgical Press, 1960, pg. 32.

Page 64: *…no peace without justice; no justice without forgiveness…*; Pope John Paul II, *Message for the Celebration of the World Day of Peace*, January 1, 2002.
If you want peace, work for justice…; Pope Paul VI, *Message for the Celebration of the Day of Peace*, January 1, 1972, also attributed to H. L. Mencken, d. 1956, perhaps a wise antidote to the Latin maxim, *if you want peace, prepare for war*.

Page 65: *As Christ was anointed…*; ICEL, *Rite of Baptism for Children*, paragraph 125.

Page 67: *My Beloved…*; Stephen Joseph Wolf, *31 Days of God's Love-Call*, idjc press, 2013, back cover.

Page 68: *To love is…*; *Catechism of the Catholic Church*, United States Conference of Catholic Bishops, 1994, 1997, #1766.

Thanks That Be   2009 Edition

It takes the help of many souls for a parish priest to do a needed five month sabbath. I am still grateful for the sabbatical, but especially for the gift of these good people:
- The parishioners of St. Stephen Catholic Community in Hermitage, Old Hickory and Mt. Juliet, Tennessee
- Parish staff: Barb Couturier, Cecilia Thomas, Youth Minister Angie Bosio, Ministries Coordinator Francie Duffield, RCIA Director Mary Craven, DRE Greg Karn, Music Director Scott Goudeau, Children Initiation Director Connie Blevins, Life Teen Band Leader Renee Campbell, Nursery Director Jaime Boyer, and Facilities Maintenance Staff Debby White, Allen Shankle, Gary Anderson, and Romey Baltz
- Theophilus Ebulueme, Head Sacristan Luis Bustillos, and Ed English

Thanks That Be

- Deacons Fred Bourland, Mickey Rose, Hans Toecker, and Jim Batcheldor
- Most Rev. David R. Choby, Bishop of Nashville and Sister Kathleen Flood, O.P.
- 2008 Parish Council *Co-chairs* John Castner & Craig Lewis; *Youth Reps*: Alec Ozminski & Ian Reding, *Worship*: Jim Simpson, Teresa Lundberg, & Cassie Kinsman; *Word*: John Reding, Erin Muldoon, & Danny Ford; *Service*: Gary Rabideau, Nicki Ballard & Jillian Hinesley; *Vocation*: Dennis Kaney, Katie Humphrey, & Catherine Black; *Evangelization*: Kathy Sullivan, Linda Norfleet, & Wil Heidorn; *Stewardship*: Kathy Walsh, Jim Mattingly, & Carly McMahon; *Secretary*: Rickie McQueen
- Priests of the Community of Passionists who assisted at Sunday Masses and Donald Webber, CP, Provincial, who gave his permission
- Ken Schmitt, daughter Annie, and the Passionist Partners of Nashville
- Tom Samoray, Director of Vocation Awareness and Young Adult Ministry
- All the Trappist monks of the Monastery of the Holy Spirit in Conyers, Georgia, including Brother Michael, Fr. James Stephen, Fr. Tom Francis, Fr. Anthony, Fr. Gerard, Abbot Francis Michael, OCSO, and the outstanding guest house staff
- The Mercy Center in Colorado Springs, CO, especially Josie Gallegos, Donna DeBartolo, Bill Winaski, Margaret Henson, and Heidi Miller
- The Institute for Continuing Theological Education (ICTE) of the North American College in Rome, especially Rev. Michael Wensing in his first semester as director, great teachers including Craig Morrison, O.Carm., James Moroney, Daniel Mueggenborg, Mark Attard, O.Carm., and what a bunch of brother priests: Joe Badding, Gerry Bechard, Jim Byers, John Capuci, Jim Carlson, Michael De Verteuil, Craig Eilerman, Don Greenhalgh, Steve Hornat, SSE, John Keefe, Joe Kelly, Bernard Kiely, Robert Lariviere, James Le, Larry McBride, Jim McClintock, Gary Meier, Michael Motta, Daniel Nascimento, Moses Ou'ou, Jay Peterson, Francis Van Pham Phuong, Gerard Pilon, James Singler, Andrzej Skizypiec, Pius To'omae and Richard Wise, tour guide extraordinaire Dr. Elizabeth Lev, and Carol Salfa
- Friends and fellow travellers on the journey: James Dylan Myers, Mike Dunne and the baseball trip gang, Brian Schieber, fellow Merton freak Ken Voiles, Rob and Maria Montini, Art Guys Michael Galbreth and Jack Massing, Rainey and Tennessee Samuel Galbreth, James F.X. Pratt, SJ, and Bill Vollmer
- And you too, Lord: Thank You!

Thanks That Be   2016 Edition

In my first parish assignment at Cathedral of the Incarnation, the pastor Bill Fleming went out of his way to encourage me to be who I am, even if that means being angry now and then. Whenever it happened, he took delight in hearing the whole story. I also wish to thank the many parishioners at the parishes of the Cathedral, Saint Stephen, Saint Henry, Saint Andrew, and Immaculate Conception Parish, who have taught me so much about being open to God's patient healing guidance. And again, you too, Lord: Thank You!

Healing happens on God's time. Lord, keep me ready.

www.ingramcontent.com/pod-product-compliance
Lightning Source LLC
Chambersburg PA
CBHW021158080526
44588CB00008B/399